BETSY DIAZ GARCIA

Au Pair life

My own history

Contents

One

Introduction

Welcome to the Au pair life My name is Betsy Diaz, and I'm very excited to write this book, I had never written a book and probably as soon as it is ready I will tell all my family and friends to read it, In this book I will tell you why I decided to become an Au pair, why I decided to leave my country, my family and my friends to go to another country and start this adventure, I will also tell you the step by step to get to where I am and how everything This experience has changed my life and my way of thinking.

I am also excited because my life experience will be reflected in this book and in the future I will be able to show my children and grandchildren, when they ask me how I managed to be the person I am, I will read this book to them because here I will write what inspired me to leave everything behind start a new life and become a better person. I hope that this book reaches many people and they are inspired by my story so that, as I did, they leave their comfort zone, change their way of thinking, see life and start from scratch, get to know another country, another language, and other people. because that expands the mind and makes you want to know more, makes you want to do it again, makes you discover who you really are and what you want to do with your life after this adventure begins.

A little about me, I have always loved traveling, seeing places, I love sunrises, sunsets, the moon and the beach, I always say that everything happens for a reason and being an Au pair I have been able to enjoy all this in a different country from where I was born It is an incredible experience, I am not very talkative and it is very difficult for me to talk to new people but once I make friends they are for a long time, I love reading and listening to music, my favorite sport is tennis and I practice it whenever I have the opportunity, I like t children and pets I hope in the future to have both.

With all those things said, let's jump right in!

How I decided to be an Au pair

Many people do not know what an Au Pair is so I will start there. An Pair is something like a baby sister but we are more like sisters or older brothers, how does it work? in my case I paid an agency to start the program they call cultural exchange, basically you go to another country you take care of children and they pay you for that but it is much more than that, you live with the family you choose and you are part of that family for one or two years, the time you decide together with the host family. You work 45 hours a week, you have 1.5 days off a week and a full weekend a month, you have 2 weeks of vacation each year and the family gives you US 500 to study and you should not pay for the stay or the food, very good right?

How did I find out that this program existed and why did I decide to do it? When I found out that this program existed, I was barely 17 years old, I was at university studying a career that I didn't really like very much, I was studying software engineering because my family has always been in the technology business and I thought it would be the most appropriate For me at that time, but one day I remember that I was in the second semester when they came to give a talk at the university, the pamphlet said something like "Do you want to know another country, learn another language and get paid for this?"

something like that I don't remember very well and as soon as I saw it I said I want it so I started to find out and inform myself what this program was and how it worked every time I read more about what it was about I liked it more

I loved the idea of getting to know other places, improving my English, expanding my mind, seeing what lies beyond, learning something new every day, but to enter the program you must meet some requirements.

The first was between 18 and 26 years old. So one could not enter so I continued in the university until I was 18. When I turned 18 I resumed the process but life had something else for me, my first love wow!just remembering it makes me sentimental it was beautiful but painful at the same time, we were together for 4 years of this relationship I learned a lot but when it ended I continued with my life project so I resumed the process to be an Au Pair, but for this I had to be studying and As I said before, I did not like my degree very much, so I left it in the fourth semester, so I looked for an economic degree that would not last more than 2 years and I began to study again in this case, it was international business,I did not like the degree very much, but I did not go to specialize in it so I decided to do it but again life had something else for me the first day of class I met a person and we had chemistry instantly but I told myself you can't fall in love because you're doing this just to be able to continue with the program and leave the country but it was inevitable and I did fall in love again, we were together for a little over a year It was a completely different relationship from the first one but from which I also learned a lot, after the relationship ended I focused again on the program and this time I managed to do it, that's why I always say that everything happens for a reason and that everything in its time Maybe if I had done the program before I wouldn't be where I am now. The following year I focused on paying for the program, meeting the necessary requirements, finishing the career I started and once and for all fulfilling that dream I had since I was 17 years old.

Three

How I found my host family

After focusing on the process, there were other requirements that I had to meet, such as having a driver's license, knowing how to swim and a first aid course. I also had to take a course on children's behavior and another if I was going to take care of babies. It was very helpful because there is always something new to learn, at the university I made a good friend, I told her about the program and she decided to do it with me, it was very helpful to have someone in this whole process, another requirement was to make a video in which I showed who I was, my family, my experience with children and because I wanted to become an AU PAIR it was a very fun experience because the cameras make me nervous and I started to laugh, it took us several months to do this, There were four countries where you can do the program USA, China, France and Germany. I chose the USA because it was the closest country and because I wanted to improve my English.

After you have all the requirements you start with the interviews with the families, I had four in total, the first was a single mother with a baby, the truth is I felt a lot of chemistry with her and I thought that this was going to be my family but after the second conversation she told me that she had found another girl that she thought was better for what she was looking for, I remember that day I became very sad, I had really liked the place where she lived and the family.

The second family was a couple with three children aged five, three and 10 months, the older children studied so I only had to take care of them in the afternoon and the baby if I had to take care of him all day, they wanted me to help them learn Spanish, I also liked this family, they had a super big house and I practically had an apartment for myself, but I didn't feel the same chemistry as with the whole family, so I continued with another interview.

I did not like the third family very much, they were a couple and two children, a girl of four and a boy of six, I had to take them to school in the morning and pick them up in the afternoon, I had everyone free in the morning to study or do whatever I wanted But even so, I did not feel confident with this family because the interview was very strange, they wrote down everything that I answered, so I decided to do another interview.

The fourth interview was like a click since I spoke with the mother I knew that this was my family, it consisted of a couple, a 17-year-old boy, a three-year-old boy and a ten-month-old baby at that time, both children were in the garden but when I arrived they were both going to be in my care, the toddler is very funny, he talks all day and has too much energy, the baby was starting to take steps and say Dada and Mama is adorable, we kept talking for several days in which I got to know more I liked the house and everything more and more, it's a good family so we decided to match.

Four

The Journey Begins

After finding the family, a few very stressful days come because you must apply for a visa to be able to travel to the USA, you have to make an appointment at the embassy and travel to the capital of my country, I remember being so nervous before the interview that I hardly fell asleep Last night, I was just thinking what if I don't get approved? this whole process will be for nothing what will I do if they don't approve it but I told myself that everything happens for a reason and if this was the right time they would approve it, and that's how it was after a few questions in the interview they approved the visa, I remember leaving the embassy still nervous and releasing the breath I didn't know I was holding, after this I called my parents and told them how excited I was because every day I was closer to that dream I had many years ago.

after the interview all the preparations for the trip begin, here they tell you that you should pack according to the season of the year, what you can and should not carry in the suitcase, you must bring something representative of your country and give it to your host parents and your hosts kids, in my case it was a little box that said Colombia on one side and inside it had typical sweets from my country and for the children t-shirts that said I love Medellin and some toy cars. before the flight I only had three weeks to say goodbye to my loved ones and pack up everything, so I started visiting my grandparents, I have six by the way, advantages of having a stepfather since I was little, they are all in different parts of the country so I took a week and a half to visit them all I only had a week and a half left so I tried to spend as much time as possible with my parents and my little brother, saying goodbye to them was the most difficult because my mom is very sentimental and always cries even on birthdays Before saying goodbye to them my little brother told me "don't leave me" my heart broke at that moment but I told him that it would only be a short time, that I would call him all the time and that soon I would be with him again, my parents were a great help because they have always supported me in my decisions and even helped me with the money to pay for the program.

After saying goodbye to my parents, the day of the flight arrived. That day I was super anxious and nervous. I was going to leave everything behind, my family, my country, my friends. I remember thinking what if this is not what I want? but again I told myself you have fought to be here for many years so don't be afraid now and I got on the plane at one in the morning but I was so anxious I wasn't sleepy, after 5 hours I was on my first stop in Miami. In Miami don't feel like you're in another country because most of the people are Latino and I heard a lot of Spanish.After an hour of waiting and another four hour flight I was finally at my destination, I had arrived in Charlotte.

when I arrived the airport was huge and being in another country I had no coverage so I had to connect to the airport network it was very funny, as soon as I arrived I wrote to my host family they were already waiting for me there I also told my parents so they wouldn't worry, after this it was to where my host family said he would wait for me it was a nice moment they had a sign that said welcome, after this we went to his house which would be my house for the next ten months because after this we would move to another state, I was happy the more places I knew the better for me, when we arrived at the house they showed me my room I liked it a lot and they also gave me a basket with personal things and some sweets.

Five

what happened after arriving

After arriving and settling in my room, I rested a bit, the rest of the week I didn't work, it was just how to adapt to what I was going to do, the hours I would take care of the children and others. The first few weeks I only took care of the baby all day and the toddler was still at school and I only took care of him for a couple of hours in the afternoon so that it would be easier for me, I would adjust and then take care of both of them all day, I had not taken care a baby in many years so I went back to review everything I had learned with my little brother, changing diapers, feeding him, putting him to bed among other things. He is a fairly easy baby, the truth is that he only cries when he is hungry, sleepy or needs a diaper change, the rest of the time he is watching TV and playing around.

It was a difficult few weeks, you realize that you are not with your family, the schedule is different here. It is an hour more which is good for me because when I leave work there it is earlier and I can talk to them, I try to call them or write to them every day.

after this my host mom gave me a routine with the kids, which we have been doing ever since, I have visited several states, one of my favorite trips was when we went to Virginia beach the hotel was in front of the sea and my room had a window immense from where I could see the sunset and sunrise from the comfort of my bed was simply beautiful.

I've been here for several months now and every day I learn new things. I even found an app to find people and play tennis and when I can't, I just play alone. I really liked being here to live this experience and learn a lot in such a short time. know and learn so that I will enjoy it to the maximum all the time that I am here.

Every celebration that I have been here has been great. I arrived a few days before Halloween to see all the decorations that were in the Halloween house. It was great they even had a ghost that was taller than me. We spent thanksgiving with some relatives of My host mom and we ate a lot.This day I made a Colombian dessert that didn't turn out very well but they liked it. Another thing that surprises me about this country is that during the festivities there is always a lot of food.

Christmas was a very nice day, my host family gave me many gifts and seeing the toddler uncover the tears with so much emotion was super fun, I gave very simple gifts to everyone that were covers for the headphones for the parents and some toys for the kids.

I have also met many people who speak Spanish, most of them are employees The one I have talked to the most is the lady who does the cleaning, one day she decided to tell me her story and her life project, she told me that she is Mexican who separated from her husband More than 20 years ago and she decided to come to the United States alone with her 3 children, who raised them here, that the oldest is already married and has 2 children and the other two are in college, she also said that before she had two jobs that she worked in a restaurant and she worked cleaning houses some days with another person but because of a crisis in the country they closed the restaurant so she decided to start sending resumes and start cleaning houses by herself and she has been doing it for ten years now too He said that this job has met very good people, even skinny people, and finally he told me that he wants to work for another ten years, save a lot and return to his country and build several houses to rent or create a party hall ace.

I really like talking to her and thinking about my future.

Six

I'm living in a movie

Why am I living in a movie? Because when you arrive in the USA everything you have seen in the movies is real, something as simple as snow, a famous restaurant or a school bus are things that I had only seen in movies and when I experience them I feel that I am living in those movies. very funny but that's how it feels, when I talk to other AU PAIR and tell them this they tell me that they feel the same and it's that everything in my country is so different that being here doesn't feel real.

Celebrations such as Valentine's Day and Thanksgiving are not seen much in my country, only some celebrate Valentine's Day and Thanksgiving is not celebrated at all, others are different, such as Halloween, here they decorate houses, cars, they do everything in a big way and the sweets that give wow, in my country only the children dress up and we go trick-or-treating at a shopping center, the super bowl here is a great event while in my country we only see the half-time show, even I don't understand why they call it football. Christmas is also different because for us it is a special occasion in which we put on new clothes, have a family dinner and celebrate together, adults open gifts on December 24 and children receive them the next morning here is a little different because all the gifts are delivered to the messages of December 25 and 24 is a normal day if they have dinner but they don't give importance to clothes, New Year for us is also special we still put on new clothes and have the family dinner, we all wait together and do something traditional

for example in my family we eat twelve grapes and make a wish with each one, most of the family always cries especially my mom who is very sentimental. Here it was different, we just had dinner and that's it, we weren't together to wait for the new year so I went to sleep a little earlier, I felt a little sad because I missed my family.

Another celebration that we don't have in Colombia is Easter, well, yes, but here they celebrate it differently. I still don't understand what the resurrection of Jesus with a rabbit and some eggs has to do with it, but it was fun to see the children look for the eggs.

Those are the celebrations that I have experienced in these months that I have been here, I look forward to those that come on July 4. I have heard that it is a very important date and it is a great celebration.

I have also realized that there are not many holidays here in Colombia, there are many and sometimes we don't even know what is celebrated, only that we don't work that day.

Next I will show you some images of my movie:

The first time I decorated a pumpkin it was exciting.

My first Halloween.

My first change of season.

My first trip, one of the most beautiful sunsets I've seen in my life.

Thanksgiving, I remember that day I ate too much.

Christmas, the tallest tree I've ever seen.

My first time knowing the snow

Trip to Savannah

My first train ride

My first Basketball game.

Sunset

Spring

I have never seen these trees before. First they are white and then green, they are beautiful.

Easter

Finally two of my favorite things together, the sunset and tennis.

Seven

How to deal with challenging situations

In some situations that I have encountered, the first few days I hardly slept because of the time change. I still did not realize that I was an hour late so I fell asleep super late so in my case I bought some patches to help me sleep better .

sometimes not understanding what other people overwhelmed me sometimes I was blank and did not know what to answer is that from one day to the next you start to see and hear everything in a different language but with the passing of the days everything is easier but There are days that it happens to me and even after all these months there are days when I am tired and I don't understand what they say to me.

What to do when children ignore you? Well in my case talking to the toddler at first he didn't listen to me but as the days went by everything was flowing better I can't deny that there are difficult days but nothing that can't be solved.

What to do when you miss home? In my case I call them almost every day but there are days when I just feel very alone and simple things like a TV show or a song make me want to cry because they talk about family but I tell myself what I should be strong for me and so that they don't see me badly and want me back, for me this has been the most difficult thing because with my family we are very close, we live together, we work together we were always together but I have used all my strength to move forward and continue with this adventure and knowing that they support me at all times helps me more, the hardest day I think was my birthday because in my house they wake me up with a song or with breakfast, the whole family calls me all the time day and night usually we get together and go to a restaurant to eat and sing the birthday or we meet at my house but this year nothing like that happened because my whole family called me but it's not the same I remember that day I went to the movies and I felt very alone, I remember crying at night but not everything was bad my host parents gave me gifts, they sang my birthday.

Christmas and New Year were also difficult because here they don't celebrate it in a big way like we do, everything is simpler and not to mention my little brother's first communion that day I also felt very sad because it is an important step in his life and I don't I was there to accompany him, my mom's birthday was another very difficult day both for me and for her because although I sent her gifts and called her she was sad because it was the first birthday we were separated, when I called her to ask if she had liked the gift she started to cry and had to hang up, I also wanted to cry but I didn't because I had to be strong for her and for me.

It also makes me sad not being able to accompany my little brother to his games because he plays soccer and I accompanied him to all the games that I could and I always remember seeing him and feeling proud of him, my mom sends me photos of the games and the scores and I always get excited, they grow up so fast.

One situation I have come across here is that they make you want to buy everything you see. Now I understand what I used to see on TV shows when they said that there are people who are compulsive hoarders, but it is so much that you see that even though you don't you need you want to buy it, I hold back a lot and only buy what I need but I have known girls who buy too many things and spend all their money on things they don't need.

Eight

What I have learned from this experience

This experience has taught me many things, I have improved my English a lot, I have seen many places but most importantly my way of seeing life I have learned that there is always something beyond that we should not be afraid of leaving everything behind and starting from scratch because With this you can transform your life and improve the quality of life for you and your loved ones, I will not deny that sometimes it is difficult and that on occasion I have felt alone, especially on special dates, such as birthdays.

Living this adventure I have missed important things like my brother's first communion and my uncle's wedding but thanks to technology I was able to accompany them from a distance. Obviously it is not the same but they are sacrifices that are made today and what a day tomorrow they will have their reward, this gave me strength.

The fact that my parents support me and are always there for me has made it a little easier and although I miss them every day they always tell me to keep going. That time goes by so fast and soon we'll be together again.

I have also met many people in this venture, I have met another AU PAIR with quite difficult stories with their host family, for example there is a girl who takes care of a child with difficulties, works more than the hours that are in the contract and is paid the same, practically They are exploiting her one day she told them that she was not going to continue with them and they gave her more work first.

is that many of the host parents do not see this program with an exchange but rather that they think they bought a babysitter.

I have heard cases ranging from the host parents not giving them food to some who kick them out of the house because they say they are going to quit, some of these cases are because the girls do not take the time to get to know the family well, rather they want to come to live the experience as quickly as possible in other cases hot parents simply lie like everything in life there are good people and people who are not, but there are also very good cases like a girl who only works a few hours in the night and he doesn't work on Fridays or weekends, it all depends on the family, that's why at the time of the interviews we must ask everything we can to make sure that we are going to go to a good family.

I don't regret being here and having learned so much and continuing to learn every day, that's why every time someone asks me I tell them to do the program without fear that this will change your life, it's a unique experience and I would like to repeat it in another country.

Soon I will get to know Texas and many more places, I will move from home and I will continue meeting incredible people and living new experiences.

Nine

Conclusion

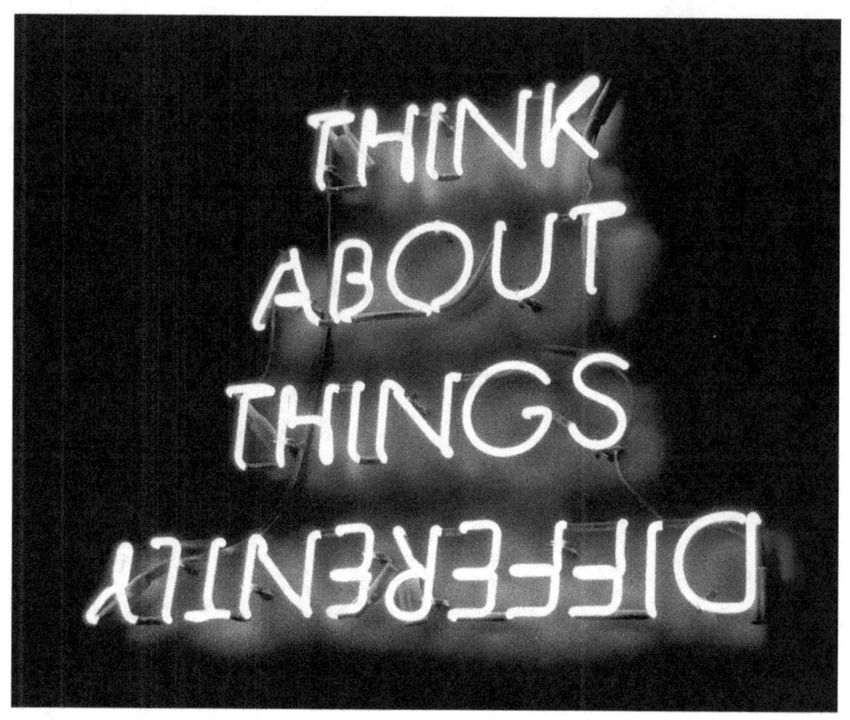

That's all, if you are young and want to live this experience, do not have any doubts, it is an opportunity to change your life, know and learn too much, if you are an adult and have children or grandchildren, tell them about this experience, it is something that will change their lives.

Thank you for reading this story, if you like it you can leave me good comments on Amazon :)

www.ingramcontent.com/pod-product-compliance
Lightning Source LLC
Chambersburg PA
CBHW070531180726

48002CB00022B/2596